EXPLORING THE STATES

Nebraska

THE CORNHUSKER STATE

by Patrick Perish

BELLWETHER MEDIA · MINNEAPOLIS, MN

Note to Librarians, Teachers, and Parents:

Blastoff! Readers are carefully developed by literacy experts and combine standards-based content with developmentally appropriate text.

Level 1 provides the most support through repetition of high-frequency words, light text, predictable sentence patterns, and strong visual support.

Level 2 offers early readers a bit more challenge through varied simple sentences, increased text load, and less repetition of high-frequency words.

Level 3 advances early-fluent readers toward fluency through increased text and concept load, less reliance on visuals, longer sentences, and more literary language.

Level 4 builds reading stamina by providing more text per page, increased use of punctuation, greater variation in sentence patterns, and increasingly challenging vocabulary.

Level 5 encourages children to move from "learning to read" to "reading to learn" by providing even more text, varied writing styles, and less familiar topics.

Whichever book is right for your reader, Blastoff! Readers are the perfect books to build confidence and encourage a love of reading that will last a lifetime!

This edition first published in 2014 by Bellwether Media, Inc.

No part of this publication may be reproduced in whole or in part without written permission of the publisher. For information regarding permission, write to Bellwether Media, Inc., Attention: Permissions Department, 5357 Penn Avenue South, Minneapolis, MN 55419.

Library of Congress Cataloging-in-Publication Data

Perish, Patrick.
 Nebraska / by Patrick Perish.
  pages cm. – (Blastoff! readers. Exploring the states)
 Includes bibliographical references and index.
 Summary: "Developed by literacy experts for students in grades three through seven, this book introduces young readers to the geography and culture of Nebraska"– Provided by publisher.
 ISBN 978-1-62617-026-1 (hardcover : alk. paper)
 1. Nebraska–Juvenile literature. I. Title.
 F666.3.P47 2014
 978.2–dc23
                                                                        2013002420

Table of Contents

Where Is Nebraska?

N
W E
S

Wyoming

Sand Hills

Colorado

Nebraska sits near the middle of the United States.
It is part of the **Midwest**. The Platte River runs through
Nebraska from west to east. Lincoln, the capital, stands
in the southeast.

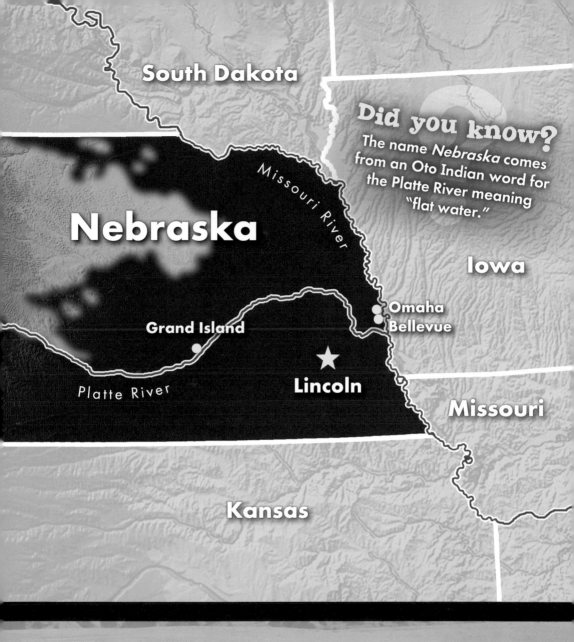

South Dakota

Nebraska

Missouri River

Did you know?
The name Nebraska comes from an Oto Indian word for the Platte River meaning "flat water."

Iowa

Omaha
Bellevue

Grand Island

★
Lincoln

Platte River

Missouri

Kansas

Nebraska's northern neighbor is South Dakota.
The Missouri River flows out of South Dakota along
Nebraska's eastern edge. It marks the border with Iowa
and Missouri. Kansas lies south of Nebraska. Colorado
borders the state to the southwest. Directly west of
Nebraska is Wyoming.

History

Native Americans first came to Nebraska thousands of years ago. In 1803, France sold the land to the United States in the **Louisiana Purchase**. The Homestead Act of 1862 let people claim their own land in Nebraska. The early settlers worked hard to survive on the plains. Nebraska became the thirty-seventh state in 1867.

the first homestead

Nebraska Timeline!

1803:	The Louisiana Purchase, which includes Nebraska, doubles the size of the United States.
1804:	Meriwether Lewis and William Clark explore the eastern edge of Nebraska. They follow the Missouri River north on their great journey west.
1840s:	Thousands of settlers cross Nebraska on the Oregon Trail to start a new life out West.
1854:	The Kansas-Nebraska Act creates the Nebraska Territory. It opens up Native American lands to white settlers.
1867:	Nebraska becomes the thirty-seventh state.
1869:	The Union Pacific Railroad out of Omaha connects to the Central Pacific Railroad out of California. This opens up the West to settlers.
1872:	Nebraska celebrates the first Arbor Day. More than a million trees are planted.
1986:	Nebraska holds the first governor election in the United States to feature only women as major candidates.

Lewis and Clark

Oregon Trail

Union Pacific Railroad

The Land

Nebraska's
Climate

average °F

spring
Low: 36°
High: 61°

summer
Low: 60°
High: 86°

fall
Low: 37°
High: 63°

winter
Low: 14°
High: 37°

Nebraska is a land of rolling hills and open plains. It has hot summers and cold winters. Powerful winds sweep across the plains. They sometimes turn into tornadoes. In the east, the soil along the Missouri River is good for farming. North-central Nebraska is covered by the grassy Sand Hills. The wide and shallow Platte River flows east across the state.

Western Nebraska is part of the **Great Plains**. The prairies here were once known as the Great American Desert. People thought they were **uninhabitable**. Today these lands are used for grazing cattle. Rising in the northwest corner of the state are the rocky hills of Nebraska's **badlands**.

The Sand Hills

In the north-central part of the state lie the rolling **dunes** of Nebraska's Sand Hills. The Sand Hills cover around 19,300 square miles (50,000 square kilometers). They make up the largest dune region in the United States.

Unlike desert dunes, the Sand Hills sit atop a large area of **groundwater**. This water allows grasses to grow and hold the dunes in place. Herds of bison used to graze here before they were wiped out by white settlers. The many streams, lakes, and **marshes** in the Sand Hills region are full of **migrating** birds each spring and fall.

fun fact

The dunes of the Sand Hills are dotted with large holes called blowouts. These occur when grasses are removed and the sand is exposed to wind.

blowout

black-tailed prairie dog

Nebraska has an abundance of wildlife. Above the river valleys, bald eagles soar in search of prey. Beavers build dams in streams throughout the state. Turtles sun themselves near ponds while dragonflies whiz by. Marshes and fields are gathering places for sandhill cranes. They dance with their mates by flapping their wings and jumping.

Did you know?

Part of the Nebraska National Forest lies in the center of the state. Its pine and cedar trees make up the largest hand-planted forest in the western half of the world.

sandhill crane

turtle

bald eagle

Out on the plains, black-tailed prairie dogs pop out of their burrows to look around. Colorful prairie chickens dart through the tall grass. At night, coyotes yip and howl to one another. Prairie rattlesnakes sleep in large dens during the winter. Hundreds of them may share a single den.

Landmarks

There are many sights to see all over Nebraska. Near the town of Alliance sits Carhenge. It is a copy of the ancient **Stonehenge** circle, except it is made out of cars. The Hastings Museum has displays of different time periods. Visitors can see models of early **sod** houses and Pawnee earth lodges.

Rising high above the western plains is Chimney Rock. This famous peak was an important landmark on the **Oregon Trail**. When settlers saw it, they knew they were getting close to the Rocky Mountains. Traces of the old trail can still be seen today.

Carhenge

Buffalo Bill's house

fun fact

Wild West showman Buffalo Bill lived in Nebraska. People can visit his old home at the Buffalo Bill State Historical Park.

Chimney Rock

Omaha is the largest city in Nebraska. More than 400,000 people call it home. It sits on the eastern border of the state along the Missouri River. The city's name comes from the Omaha Native American tribe and means "upstream people."

In the 1860s, Omaha became an important city for transportation. The Union Pacific Railroad connected it to Sacramento, California. Today, visitors can learn all about the railroads of the Old West at the Durham Museum. It is housed in an old train station. The Henry Doorly Zoo and Aquarium is another favorite Omaha attraction. Its desert exhibit features rattlesnakes, ocelots, wallabies, and more.

Henry Doorly Zoo

fun fact
The Henry Doorly Zoo is home to the world's largest indoor desert!

Working

Did you know?

Over nine-tenths of Nebraska's land is used for farming and ranching. This is more than any other state.

Farming and ranching are important all over Nebraska. Farmers grow corn, hay, wheat, and soybeans. Areas such as the Sand Hills are perfect for grazing cattle. Nebraska is one of the nation's top producers of beef, pork, and chicken. Factory workers package the meat. They also turn grains into flour, cereal, and animal feed.

Since the first railroad entered Nebraska, transportation has provided many jobs. Today, Nebraskans haul goods across the state by train and truck. Workers in the southwest dig for oil and natural gas. Many Nebraskans have **service jobs**. They work in hotels, restaurants, and visitor centers.

Where People Work in Nebraska

government
14%

services
72%

manufacturing
9%

farming and
natural resources
5%

Playing

Did you know?
Nebraska is called the Cornhusker State after the college football team.

Memorial Stadium

Nebraskans love to be active, especially outdoors. The state parks offer beautiful trails for hiking and cross-country skiing. People like to bird-watch in the wetlands. Many Nebraskans also enjoy hunting for white-tailed deer and grouse. Fishers pull bass and catfish from the lakes and streams.

fishing

Memorial Stadium in Lincoln is
home to the Cornhuskers college
football team. The school colors are red and white.
The crowds of fans are known as the "sea of red." When
the stadium is full, it has more people than any city in
Nebraska except Lincoln and Omaha.

Food

meatloaf

fun fact

A Nebraska legend says popcorn was discovered one hot summer when the kernels began popping off the cobs.

As a major farming state, Nebraska is serious about its food. Beef, corn, and wheat are all key parts of a Nebraska diet. German-speaking Russians brought the *runza* sandwich when they came to the state. This pocket of bread is stuffed with meat, cabbage, and onions. As in other Midwestern states, pot roast, meatloaf, and potato dishes are common meals.

Popcorn and popcorn balls are other favorite local foods. A berry pudding called *wojapi* is a **traditional** dessert of the Plains Indians. It is often eaten with **fry bread**. Native Americans and early settlers also ate jerky. This dried and salted meat kept for a long time without spoiling.

Popcorn Balls

Ingredients:

- 1 1/4 cups sugar
- 1 1/4 cups brown sugar
- 1/2 cup light corn syrup
- 2/3 cup water
- 1 tablespoon butter
- 14 cups popped natural popcorn
- 1 1/4 teaspoons salt

Directions:

1. Heat sugars, corn syrup, and water in a saucepan. Stir until sugar is dissolved.

2. Add butter and continue cooking without stirring until the mixture reaches 240°F.

3. Put the popped popcorn into a large bowl and sprinkle with salt.

4. Pour the hot syrup over the popcorn and mix well with a spoon.

5. Grease your hands and quickly shape into small balls.

6. Place popcorn balls on a greased pan to cool. When cool, wrap in wax paper.

Festivals

Taste of Omaha

The Kool-Aid drink mix was invented in Hastings, Nebraska. Each year, the town hosts Kool-Aid Days to celebrate. The festival includes music, contests, and the world's largest Kool-Aid stand. The Taste of Omaha is a three-day food festival in June. People sample tasty dishes from chefs and restaurants across the city.

world's largest
Kool-Aid stand

powwow
dance

Nebraskaland Days is a
June festival held in North Platte.
It features parades, concerts, and **rodeos**. Cowboys and
cowgirls compete in bull riding, barrel racing, and calf
roping. At **powwows**, people celebrate Native American
culture with traditional songs and dances.

In 1862, the U.S. government passed the Homestead Act. This allowed people to claim and improve a piece of land in the West. Trees were scarce when early settlers arrived on the Nebraska plains. The settlers had to find other building materials for their homes.

two-story sod house

The roots of prairie grasses held dirt together in thick mats of sod. Settlers cut these mats into bricks and stacked them to make sod houses. A special plow made cutting sod easier. Sod houses stayed cool during the summer. In winter, they kept heat from stoves inside. Nebraskans today are proud of their history and the **pioneer** spirit of those who settled their state.

Fast Facts About Nebraska

Nebraska's Flag

The Nebraska flag features the state seal set in a field of blue. The seal shows scenes of Nebraska life. These include a train passing in front of mountains and a steamboat traveling down the Missouri River. The seal also shows a blacksmith working near a wheat field. Above the scenes is a banner displaying the state motto.

State Flower
goldenrod

State Nicknames:	The Cornhusker State The Beef State
State Motto:	"Equality Before the Law"
Year of Statehood:	1867
Capital City:	Lincoln
Other Major Cities:	Omaha, Bellevue, Grand Island
Population:	1,826,341 (2010)
Area:	77,349 square miles (200,333 square kilometers); Nebraska is the 16th largest state.
Major Industries:	farming, manufacturing, transportation, services
Natural Resources:	farmland, rivers, oil, natural gas, cement
State Government:	49 senators
Federal Government:	3 representatives; 2 senators
Electoral Votes:	5

State Bird
western meadowlark

State Animal
white-tailed deer

Glossary

badlands—dry, hilly lands that have been worn down by wind and water

dunes—hills of sand

fry bread—fried dough; Native Americans first made fry bread from government food supplies when they were forced off their lands.

Great Plains—a region of flat or gently rolling land in the central United States; the Great Plains stretch over about one-third of the country.

groundwater—water held underground in the soil and rock

Louisiana Purchase—a deal made between France and the United States; it gave the United States 828,000 square miles (2,144,510 square kilometers) of land west of the Mississippi River.

marshes—wetlands with grasses and plants

Midwest—a region made up of 12 states in the north-central United States

migrating—traveling from one place to another, often with the seasons

native—originally from a specific place

Oregon Trail—a route extending more than 2,000 miles (3,219 kilometers) from Missouri to Oregon; pioneers traveled west on the trail between 1840 and 1860.

pioneer—a person who was among the first to explore or settle in a place

powwows—celebrations of Native American culture that often include singing and dancing

rodeos—events where people compete at tasks such as bull riding and calf roping; cowboys once completed these tasks as part of their daily work.

service jobs—jobs that perform tasks for people or businesses

sod—the top layer of soil held together by the roots of grasses

Stonehenge—an ancient circle of large stones near Salisbury, England

traditional—relating to a custom, idea, or belief handed down from one generation to the next

uninhabitable—unable to support life

To Learn More

AT THE LIBRARY

Monnig, Alex. *Nebraska Cornhuskers*. Minneapolis, Minn.: ABDO Pub. Co., 2013.

Sanford, William R. *Buffalo Bill Cody: Courageous Wild West Showman*. Berkeley Heights, N.J.: Enslow Publishers, 2013.

Weatherly, Myra. *Nebraska*. New York, N.Y.: Children's Press, 2009.

ON THE WEB

Learning more about Nebraska is as easy as 1, 2, 3.

1. Go to www.factsurfer.com.

2. Enter "Nebraska" into the search box.

3. Click the "Surf" button and you will see a list of related Web sites.

With factsurfer.com, finding more information is just a click away.

Index

The images in this book are reproduced through the courtesy of: Judd Patterson/ Getty Images, front cover
(bottom), pp. 14-15; (Collection)/ Prints & Photographs Division/ Library of Congress, pp. 6, 27 (small); John
Kropewnicki, p. 7 (left); Wweagle, p. 7 (middle); Antonio Abrignani, p. 7 (right); Tom Till/ SuperStock, pp. 8-9;
George Burba, pp. 10-11, 14 (bottom); Kody M. Unstad, p. 10 (small); Lightpoet, pp. 12-13; Tania Thomson,
p. 13 (top); Brian Lasenby, p. 13 (middle); Sekar B, p. 13 (bottom); Naaman Abreu, p. 14 (top); Walter Bibikow/
Getty Images, pp. 16-17; Bill Grant/ Alamy, p. 17 (small); Pasquale Mingarelli/ Alamy, p. 18; Exactostock/
SuperStock, p. 19 (small); John S. Peterson/ Icon SMI AYA/ Newscom, pp. 20-21; MidwestWilderness, p. 21
(small); Canadapanda, p. 22; Mr. Surakit Harntongkul, p. 22 (small); James R. Martin, p. 23 (small); Gregory L.
Davenport/ Davenport Projex Photography, pp. 24-25; Matt Dixon, p. 25 (top); Wdeon, p. 25 (bottom); Glenda,
pp. 26-27; Pakmor, p. 28 (top); Le Do, p. 28 (bottom); Tony Campbell, p. 29 (left); Martha Marks, p. 29 (right).